# The Intergenerational Impact: How Successful Family Environments Perpetuate Success and Generational Wealth

Success and wealth often seem like distant aspirations, achievable only through extraordinary effort and luck.

However, upon closer examination, it becomes apparent that success and wealth are not merely products of individual endeavors but are deeply intertwined with the environments in which individuals are raised.

In particular, the role of family environment in shaping success and perpetuating generational wealth cannot be overstated.

This book explores the mechanisms through which successful family environments foster achievement and prosperity across generations.

# 1. **Cultural Capital and Values Transmission**

Successful family environments are characterized by the transmission of cultural capital and values that prioritize education, hard work, and resilience.

Children raised in such environments are imbued with a sense of ambition and determination from an early age.

They are taught to value education as a means of upward mobility and to approach challenges with a growth mindset.

This transmission of cultural capital sets the stage for future success by instilling the attitudes and behaviors necessary to navigate the complexities of the modern world.

## 2. Access to Resources and Opportunities

Wealth begets wealth, and successful family environments often provide access to a plethora of resources and opportunities that set individuals on the path to success.

Whether it's access to quality education, mentorship, or financial capital, children raised in affluent families are endowed with advantages that facilitate their personal and professional growth.

These resources serve as springboards, enabling individuals to capitalize on their talents and aspirations in ways that might not be possible otherwise.

## 3. **Social Networks and Support Systems**

Beyond material resources, successful family environments also offer robust social networks and support systems that play a crucial role in fostering success.

From familial connections to influential mentors, individuals raised in such environments benefit from access to a diverse array of contacts who can provide guidance, support, and opportunities for advancement.

These networks serve as conduits for information and social capital, opening doors to career opportunities, investment ventures, and collaborative partnerships.

## 4. **Intergenerational Knowledge Transfer**

Success is often built upon the foundations laid by previous generations, and successful family environments excel in the transfer of intergenerational knowledge and expertise.

Whether it's a family business passed down through generations or the sharing of entrepreneurial insights, the wisdom accumulated over time serves as a blueprint for navigating the complexities of the marketplace.

By learning from the successes and failures of their predecessors, individuals in successful family environments are better equipped to make informed decisions and capitalize on emerging opportunities.

## 5. **Emotional Intelligence and Resilience**

Success is not solely contingent upon intellectual prowess or financial acumen but also on emotional intelligence and resilience.

Successful family environments cultivate these qualities by fostering a supportive and nurturing atmosphere where individuals are encouraged to develop self-awareness, empathy, and coping mechanisms.

Through the cultivation of emotional intelligence, individuals are better equipped to navigate setbacks and challenges, emerging stronger and more resilient in the face of adversity.

## 6. **Legacy Building and Philanthropy**

Beyond personal success, successful family environments often emphasize the importance of legacy building and philanthropy.

By instilling a sense of responsibility towards their communities and society at large, individuals raised in such environments are motivated to leverage their resources and influence for the greater good.

Whether through charitable giving, social entrepreneurship, or community engagement, they actively contribute to the betterment of society while simultaneously solidifying their family's legacy for future generations.

In conclusion, successful family environments play a pivotal role in perpetuating success and generational wealth by providing a fertile ground for personal and professional development.

Through the transmission of cultural capital, access to resources and opportunities, robust social networks, intergenerational knowledge transfer, cultivation of emotional intelligence, and emphasis on legacy building, these environments equip individuals with the tools and mindset necessary to thrive in an increasingly competitive world.

By recognizing and harnessing the power of family environments, we can pave the way for a more equitable and prosperous future where success is not just a privilege but a possibility for all.

Please use the next few pages for your notes and debates.

www.ingramcontent.com/pod-product-compliance
Lightning Source LLC
Chambersburg PA
CBHW030108230526
45471CB00003B/1311